Solastalgia

*Poems of Reflection
and Remembrance*

Brian McManus

Best wishes,

Bjmcmanus

First published 2021 by The Hedgehog Poetry Press

Published in the UK by
The Hedgehog Poetry Press
5, Coppack House
Churchill Avenue
Clevedon
BS21 6QW

www.hedgehogpress.co.uk

ISBN: 978-1-913499-64-8

9 8 7 6 5 4 3 2 1

A CIP Catalogue record for this book is available from the
British Library.

Contents

If you are one of the many people who have suffered grievous loss, or are one of those people who have protected and supported us and prevented such a loss, then these poems are for you

INTRODUCTION

From the Lockerbie Air Disaster through to the present day Covid pandemic and everything in between, the work in this volume reflects on a time in our lives when we have all had to deal exponentially with the often complex and challenging vagaries of life, love, extreme loss and debilitating uncertainty in our once predictable and understandable world.

Reflecting, and remembering, is important. However, although we wouldn't wish to disassociate ourselves from our past, neither should we mourn it. There is a balance to be struck between paying homage, and around identifying the questions and the answers we need to work with as we move forward. The moment we are in is the only life we have. So, let us remember and reflect then one last time on the aftermath of some of the soul-crushing events of our recent lifetimes, and pay our final respects to those innocent souls who were caught up in the tumult. Then, the old days are the old days, let's move on.

The early incarnation of some of these poems were first published some years ago but are now sadly out of print. I've reproduced some of them, and rewritten or updated others. The majority however are published here for the first time. I hope you find them of some solace, and of some value.

Thank you for your interest,

and best wishes.

Brian.

(14 April 2021)

SONGS OF PRAISE

First published in the 1995
Bridport prize-winners anthology

They came to sing their songs and praise his name,
and took their seats in rows of polished yew,
but nothing in their lives would be the same.

Outside, the clouds replete with salty rain,
the restless heavens waiting for their cue,
they came to sing their songs and praise his name.

The preacher rolls the dice to start the game,
as plates of burnished silver claim their due,
but nothing in their lives would be the same.

The stars resigned to hang their heads in shame,
unable to prevent their passing through,
they came to sing their songs and praise his name.

The preacher stokes the fire, fans the flame,
replenishes, recharges faith anew,
but nothing in their lives would be the same.

The heavens and the stars were not to blame,
seek to understand the one who knew.
They came to sing their songs and praise his name,
but nothing in their lives would ever be the same.

WHERE A HOUSE ONCE STOOD

If you listen closely you can hear
the sound of
 children playing,
  neighbours chatting,
   roses growing;
secret cans of beer
in potting shed.

Drifting strands of breeze pick out
the sound of
 dinner cooking,
  church bells ringing,
   grandad snoring;
tilted boater
shading sleepy head.

Outside broadcast vans record
the sound of
 hurried briefings,
  hourly updates,
   numbing silence;
where a house once stood,
now lie the dead.

THE GIRL I NEVER MET

Short-listed for the 1994
Rhyme International prize

Yes, I remember finding her that
day. I saw her, unexpected, as I
walked in gardens, where children

used to play. She'd fallen on a bed
of frosted rock. Possessions littered
sadly all around. I turned and gulped

the air against the shock. I stood in
humble silence as I found the fading
light reflected in her eyes. An angel,

cast unwanted to the ground. Later,
as we choked on all their lies, their
platitudes, their sparsely-mouthed

regrets, we found that as hope lives,
it also dies. My life revolves around
her memory yet ..

.. the girl I once picked up,
but never met.

I CRIED FOR YOU TODAY

Since you've been gone, the hours grow long,
the days run into nights. I mourn the love we
shared before the drawing down of light. I miss
the touch of your caress, the whisper of your

breath. A prelude to our tenderness, our love,
which bled to death. I'm lonely now, I'm tired.
So cold. I hug the candlelight, and dream the
dreams which bound us then as we lay close

at night. It haunts my every memory, that love
I live without. Those sun-soaked days, those
sleep-starved nights .. I snuff the candle out.
I close my eyes. I see your face. I gently trace

your lips. I sense your raw emotion pulse beneath
my fingertips. I lie awake, while salty tears pearl
slowly from my eyes. Your bedside photograph
records the day before you died. You're happy now,

I know you are, I cried for you today. You've found
a place to rest your head where gods and angels play.
Time slips by so quietly, the little things I miss, the
scent of you at daybreak, and your tender, loving, kiss.

THINK OF BEING THEM

"Why should I let the "toad" work
squat on my life?" (Philip Larkin)

"I dodge the "toad" whenever I can,
it wouldn't suit me ..
up and down those lines to the city ..
five days a week to infinity." (R.A.Maitre)

Going home at night, the booze would mask the taste of death.
The dawn's delay a multi-purpose cloak. It fitted well our sense
of disillusionment. Humbled, dolefully sifting through lost lives.

No need to dodge the toad, or squeeze up on the Piccadilly line.
No fighting in the scrum, no mercy shown. No holding, touching,
muted. Not a sound. No warning given. Searching, no life found ..

.. no need to offer them your arm, old Toad,
they've long since marched down cemetery road.

LAST ORDERS

Jimmy paused, then grimaced, tried to smile,
through half-a-dozen stumps which passed

for teeth. We raised a glass, tried to reconcile
the wrecking ball which laid waste our belief

in moral's right to triumph over wrong. The
bonfire of our certainties. Our trust dissipated,

squandered, all along just kicked around, left
lying in the dust. That night we drank in honour

of old friends, we'd grown to know like family.
More beers? Perhaps we thought the booze

might put an end to what had gone before?
There were some tears. We'd tramped around

our gruesome netherworld, our mindset not to
be the first to speak of nagging fears or worries.

None of us could bring ourselves to say it. Do
you see? Well anyway, that's how it's meant to

be, but what we saw left plenty room for doubt.
Later, when the Salvage Corps had left? 600 bags

of homeless putrid flesh. Before we said *adieu* to
restless days and sleepless nights, we had a wander

down to visit at the crater, one last time, and marked
the desolation all around with rolls of six by fours.

They'd always be our poignant record, framed without
the sound of life or laughter ..

*.. here's to you old friends, we'll always
share this sacred common ground.*

UNDERGROUND

I lie beneath a train. I cannot feel my legs. Questions, pulsing
through my brain. I reach out for the threads of consciousness,

vitality, the will to stay alive. I concentrate, I try my best, hope
that I'll survive. I'm choking now, can't catch my breath, blood

now fills my lungs. Metallic taste, then salty sweet, it's coursing
down my throat. I know it's time. I close my eyes. I see a bright

blue sky. Our perfect beach, lapping waves, my happy smiling guy.
Now in a church, I love my dress. The kids stand at my side. Tired,

though I feel at peace, I don't feel any pain. One final thing, before
I go, you shouldn't all feel sad. It's what it is. Just promise you'll get

on and live your lives. Today will pass, as will the fear, the heartache
and the strife. I love you all, please love me back, time to say goodbye ..

.. laters x.

CHASING BUTTERFLIES

I sensed your longing. Lilies staked tonight
astride your tortured body, sultry-sweet

but out of reach. I'd sometimes fly a kite
on twisted thermals, looking to complete

a symbiotic, coupled state of mind. Where
we could play and grow, that promised

land, a place we'd never get to. Now I find
a million questions in a grain of sand.

I loved her then, and now, I love her still.
I sang her praises, played up to my role.

I'll love her every single day until the
black dog howls and lacerates my soul.

And then? I'll simply love her even more.
I'll clear the darkest corners of my mind,

and love her like I've never loved before,
tap-dancing on the eyelids of the blind.

That vastitude of screaming, sordid pain,
those tortured lows, no iridescent highs.

The emptiness of nothing left to gain,
our veins wide open, chasing butterflies.

CROSSING AT AMBER

The warmth of the ancient chapel
is fuelled by big, cranky radiators.
The translucent world outside the
window where she once lived and

happily thrived, is eerily bathed in
opaque, yellow light. Snow begins
to drift and settle in the lee of the
sparse, thorny native hedge, crude

metaphor for life's impermanence
and often traumatic consequences
of unnerving continuity and change.
A hymn of remembrance resonates

from the small town choir as bereft
mourners rise, and take their leave.
As they exit solemnly, thanking the
pastor, snowflakes continue to fall,

pure and unsullied, but naive. They
bond together as crystalline brother
and sister, and resolutely set about
their task. Working together at heavy

hearts and limp spirits, they will dress
threadbare flowerbeds, mourners and
grateful town's people in a comforting
blanket of anonymity. Quiet descends ..

She has passed away. In her life we
embraced her. In her death we crave
no weeping or pain. We give thanks
for her freedom from a world in which
we are forever fated to cross at amber.

THE CURIOSITY OF QUIET PLACES

Although we meet now face-to-face, our travels
in this quiet place seem not to soothe. Let's try

to find a simpleness, a peace of mind. Our time is
spent beguiled by talk of then and now. Most days

we walk a melancholy path. Still strife. Still searching for
the happy life. Our trust, unpacked, our faith, on show.

No vengeful lust, nor ruthless foe. A kinship forged by
cruel decree. Love's gyroscope can set us free. Dear

troubled friend, let's cultivate a different story, solve our
plight. A sacred tale, a means to cope, a sense of freedom,

not of blight. The love we lost, the strength we've found. A
better life, suffused with hope. Godless deaths? - out of scope.

SUBJUGATION

Dark, heavy skies shroud cold grey days
as time-frozen tableaux mirror cut winter

blooms, mourning, at the feet of the dead.
Watery winter light licks rough-hewn stone,

as find drilled marble silently counts out the
Roll of Honour. Never cowed, not forgotten,

the dead of this war. Bear witness, in years
when we may not, for patriots and heroes,

innocents, and fools. Harbour your chronicle
with stout heart, against the cynical tyranny

of generations, and attest to our pleading, which
falls, weary and beaten, on barren, stony ground.

TRANSTEMPORAL

Travelling down on bitter, icy mornings, a comfort blanket
of perennial darkness would ease us gently into the pre-dawn.
The journey's dip and sway grew heavy on our shuttered eyes,
as faint metallic lullabies crackled forlornly around the silent van.

As we approached the summit, a bleak rolling haar might descend
upon the carriageway, shrouding us in its deep, purposeful sense
of foreboding. Then, as time-travellers, we'd retreat through the
centuries, as an ancient torchlit procession bore down upon us,

menacingly. Chanting softly, burning clubs thrust high into the
deepening gloom, the low growl of the fog shrouded line snakes
ever closer. Now, back on the open road, tense knuckled, as the
motorway chargers flash past. Later, us, steeling ourselves ..

.. for our new normal

REFLECTIONS

(i) I think of then, and how it must have been.
The aura of their presence haunts me, still.
Lately, time seems wandered. The wizard's
glass reflects the tragic scene. Hands, never
clean, as the sisters screech their prophecies.
Now, as I lie at night, I feel the sudden chill
of whispered breath, behind me; as I dream.

(ii) Aviation fuel, the stench regales my senses.
Thirty two years on the crater is filled in now,
the scar is always present. Lifeless, I tagged
them with a label. Thirty two years on, salty
tears meet single malt, their spirits travel with
me. On the longest night, I walk around their
garden. Thirty two years on, salute once more
my cherished friends, lives embalmed in ornate
stone. Time, such an inconsequential construct.

UNCONSCIONABLE

Inaction, dearth of vision. The planet
burns, the oceans swell and grow.

Prevarication, rants, lies. Our temporary
time on earth abused. No scope for further

time torn off unused. When Pangaea rifted,
the earth was torn apart. Continental drift

continues to this day. Schisms still widen.
Life still decays. Six degrees more heat

and our lives will turn to dust. Tempestites
recount questions, not solutions, in our

cosmic evolution. In aeons yet to come,
Pangaea Proxima, an extirpated world,

a toxic conurbation, no hope for our salvation?
It's in our hands, this surely isn't all there is.

RUNNING ON EMPTY

Locked down. Worried, nervous. Tense, breathless.
Past caring, beyond mourning. Defeated, just dying,

inside. Those we cherished, gone. Forever. Our lives
and futures? Full of holes. No hugging, no laughter.

No-one left to love, or to love us. No more memories
to create, nothing left to build. Our useful days behind

us, everything on hold. What's left? Determination,
resolution, the balls to see it through. Otherwise ..

.. a world of emptiness, and slowly growing old.

THE GAME

To play the game we needed complex
rules, of sorts. We had no say around

those rules. Their esoteric brand of
tortured thought, deluded currency of

fools. Despite it all, we've tried to play
the game, and shuffled in our chains

along the queue. Our anguished lives
were never quite the same, our time

being lined with loneliness and gloom.
The Songbird starts to weep, the Jester

nails his colours to the floor. Now, as
we waken from our toxic sleep, we're
queuing to march through the exit door ..

*.. the Karma man takes stock, and then takes aim,
the lyrics change, the song remains the same.*

AFFIRMATION

Learn how to let go
Be calm in this frantic world
Keep your own counsel
Resolve to trust the process
Create eunoia and belief

Listen first, then speak
Be accessible, build bonds
Stumble, yes. Fall, no.
Pick yourself up, move forward
Boundaries, not barriers

Make yourself worth being
Build resilience and strength
Travel honestly
Proceed with integrity
Offer caring and comfort

If life is a dance
Emotion is the music
Be present always
Pay attention, on purpose
Live your life in the moment

We are all artists
A multi-coloured palette
We paint with language
Affirmed by our actions
The joy is in the journey

QUALIA

In our precious journey, life pushes, pulls,
and cajoles, with intent and with purpose.

Defined by luminescence, distilled by
transcendence; purified and held by love.

Each authentically lived life an ever evolving
work of art. Enjoy making your art. *Be your*

art. Share of yourself, gloriously. Be present.
Contribute generously with each sculpted step

you take. Spiritual evolution finds itself. Take
the time to acknowledge your debt, with grace.

Having found yourself, live your one wonderful
life one precious moment at a time. Remember,

death is not an end stop. Work to burnish future
lives with profound care, and with clear, raw light.

ANTECEDENTS

How we live measures our own nature, he said,
and would say still. That subtle disconnect from

womb to tomb, and every day those threads
grow tussocky; slow-tangled. Pause, reflect

on all those half-framed thoughts which slipped
away, the deeds and actions chalked which never

lived, no move from light to luminosity, that spark
we never glimpsed, nor life to give. Old sins cast

the longest shadows, it's said, so here we are.
Bracelets round our hearts, and cloistered minds

patrolled by fear and dread, of being someone
different. Let's start to march with purpose down

our one-way street, caps set against the dying
of the light. The cobbles bare and rude beneath
our feet ..

.. let's make our visit; curse those restless nights.

COMMON BONDS

If we strive to suffer silently
and stay our troubled souls.
If we contain our deepest
pain yet work towards our

goals. If we can fight back
acid tears and choke off
strangled sobs, tormented
by the knowledge that our

loved ones walk with gods.
If we can seek salvation for
the men who caused this loss,
if we can bear this heavy load

as though we bore a cross. If
we refuse to stoop our backs
and to the wind won't bend, do
we then merit taunts and jibes

from those who'd call us friends?
As the stars descend from heaven
and our highest symbols pale. As
the sway of nature falters and our

trust in reason fails. As we take a
knee for days gone by and our
tears become a flood ..

*.. remember then what common bonds
are forged through light and love.*

ACKNOWLEDGEMENT

Thanks are due to my publisher Mr Mark Davidson who despite the most trying of circumstances has managed to keep the poetry plates spinning and get these words out into the world. 'Great job sir, well played!